# Walking Through the Fire

James Burkett

Copyright © 2018 James Burkett

Cover art by Kay Burkett

All rights reserved.

ISBN-10:1986508315
ISBN-13: 978-1986508315

FOR MY FAMILY

# Table of Contents

Life in Between 3
Birth and Death 4
Wind 5
reflected light 6
Night Over the Lake 7
Darkness 8
Morning in the Woods 9
Sky and Lake 10
Walking Through the Fire 12
The Girls Who Picked Peaches 14
Old Things 17
The Village Dump 18
Trip to the Campo 19
remember poverty 25
March of Terror 28
One Breath Away 29
Night Without End 30
Life 32
Seventh Cousins 33
Tribe 34
When an Old Man Dies a Library Burns 36
Mervin 37
Quietus 38
Looking Out the Window 40

To make a beginning one must make an end. The beginning is at the end.

# Life In Between

The day I was born
Is not in my memory.
My folks tell the tale.

The day that I die
I shall never remember.
You tell the story.

The days in between
Are alive in memory.
I spin the yarn.

James Burkett

## Birth and Death

Enter the world wailing
All rejoice.
Leave the world rejoicing
All wail.

## **wind**

watch the wind blow
in waves across the horizon
sometimes purple
sometimes gray
howling through the trees
like the prison guard
moving life along its course

James Burkett

# reflected light

in the west the setting sun
red, orange and gold
all that lies in sunlight's path
gleams in rich color

suddenly the east side of a tree
bursts brilliant
with the colors
of the setting sun

# Night Over the Lake

Sunsets are golden
Over the lake of blue
Trees stand like skeletons

Geese swim nonchalantly
Evenings dimming light
Noisily chattering

Soon darkness will cover
And the lake turns to black
Night rule commandeers

James Burkett

# Darkness

The season of darkness approaches.
Afternoon light succumbs
To brilliant sunsets
And gives way to the enveloping dark.

We shudder as the darkness casts
Its shadow of vulnerability;
And we shrink
From the imagined evil.

We cling to the hope
That the light will return,
Ignorant of the fact
We need the darkness.

## Morning in the Woods

I sat on a log by the brook
in the still of the morning
regaled by the symphony of the woods:

Insects singing,
a chorus of cardinals,
woodpeckers keeping beat,
little peepers tweeting,
and the crows holding jury,

while leaves drift to the ground
some dancing through the air
some plummeting with elaborate splash.

the blue aster and golden rod
in full costume
at the height of their bloom
undulate with bees.

James Burkett

# Sky and Lake

Blue sky
Blue lake

Gray sky
Gray lake

Black sky
Black lake

Calm sky
Calm lake

Angry sky
Angry lake

Sunset in sky
Sunset in lake

Moon in sky
Moon in lake

Sky and lake are one.

Moments are the mileposts of life – sometimes we influence them, more often we become part of them and allow them to influence us.

James Burkett

# Walking Through the Fire

I went to a cross country meet.  My granddaughter
runs on the varsity team for her school.
The meet had thousands of participants
from western New York schools.
There were thousands of spectators.  Schools from
every division in the state participated,
each competing in their own class.
A different race began every twenty minutes.
Varsity girls, seeded schools, class A,
the 23rd race of the day beginning on time to the minute –
3:53 in the afternoon – the race I came to watch.

Cross country is said to be the only sport where
the spectators get nearly as much exercise
as the participants.
From the parking lot, a mile to the meet site
taking place in a "natural bowl"
beside the Genesee River.
Both start and finish happened on the green of the bowl.
Runners ran first into the woods on one side,
crossed the green and into the woods on the other side.
It made watching easy, but demanded
a lot of walking.  Cross the green at one end,
then cross again at the other end, then to the finish.
One had to scurry
to see one's favorite runner.

*The routine remains the same as when my kids were running
cross country.  Be at the start line yelling for them to begin
strong, Next to the top of the hill before they entered the
pasture encouraging them on, but stay put until they come out
of the pasture yelling for them to pass the runner in front of*

*them, and finally to the finish line urging them to sprint the last 100 yards, all required a vigorous trot from one vantage point to the next to be in time to see the runner pass.*

Cross country running is a brutal sport – in high school run as fast as you can for three miles and cross the finish line in less than twenty minutes if you are a girl – less than fifteen minutes if you are a boy. It requires a lot of training and perseverance.

My granddaughter wore
a long sleeve warm up tee shirt.
The saying on the back –
"What matters most is how well you walk through the fire."

Today she ran the course in 19 minutes and 33 seconds.

James Burkett

# The Girl Who Picked Peaches

A girl came picking peaches from the trees across the lane.
The same girl who picked peaches several weeks ago
when they were green and hard.
A winsome lass with a quick smile and toddler, Henry,
who informed me that he was two years old.
She picked a half basket of peaches and cut
twigs and leaves from the tree
in her loose fitting, linen smock, that revealed
her small firm breasts
when she leaned over to place peaches
and twigs in the basket.
I asked her what she had done
with the peaches she picked that were not ripe.
She smiled and replied
she made salsa,
"It was very tart," she concluded.

Nimbly she jumped onto a bench dragged
from the backyard picnic table,
took a peach in her small delicate hand,
and plucked it from the tree. She apologetically allowed
that she had picked about all the peaches she could reach.
About a peck of peaches remained high in the tree.
I told her I would bring my step ladder tomorrow
and pick the peaches in the upper part of the tree.
We talked about the peach trees.
She thought they were beautiful.
I told her they bore peaches in abundance two years ago
when I helped the previous owner thin them before the
fruit ripened. The remaining fruit developed
into larger and tastier peaches.
We both knew the trees bore no peaches last year.

An early cold snap froze the blossoms.
She told me that she was the sister of the owner
of the house, which without saying
implicitly gave her the right to pick the peaches and prune
the twigs and leaves which she intended
to make into a tea.  She is an herbalist. Her sky blue eyes
twinkled as she explained that she plans to use the twigs
and leaves in her practice.  She mentioned she had
attended the school of massage.
"But I no longer practice," she noted.
Henry needed attention. I needed to clean the camper.
Our conversation ended.

Peach tea made from the twigs and leaves of the tree
       soothes and
              calms.

James Burkett

Our lives are not about the goals we set or the final achievements we attain, but about the way in which we live.

## Old Things

Old things and antiques
Have value to some
But old things decay
And turn into crumb
Loss of things valuable
Cause all to be glum
That which was beautiful
Has became a slum

Old people like old things
Wither and decay
But with love and affection
One just may
Find a jewel of wisdom
That to all can convey
Bright hope for tomorrow
And enlightenment today

James Burkett

# The Village Dump

They come from village nearby.
They come from surrounding country side.
They gather on Saturday mornings –
mostly men, but a few women –
in the driveway off the township road
filing in and out of the nearby shack
to warm themselves in the winter
or find shade cover from the hot summer sun.

They greet as old friends are wont to do
and inquire about the well being of each other.
They talk about the latest happenings in the community
and opine the right and wrong
of the course taken by local leaders.
They revel in the prowess of the local sports teams
and reminisce about when they were the stars.
They speculate who will be married,
repine about who has passed,
deplore those who have caused trouble,
and discuss the general gossip of the area.

When their exchanges conclude
they set out to accomplish the tasks
for which they gathered –
sorting the cardboard from the paper
and that from the plastics, glass, and metals
to be placed in the appropriate recycle bins,
and finally to lug large bags of trash to the compactor
where the dross is heaved into the abyss
to be crushed and hauled to the landfill.

## Trip to the Campo

### 1

Leaving the city east on CA 1,
Pan American Highway,
route to South America,
the lush green, tropical countryside belies
stark poverty enveloped in its luxurious arms.
Hot humid weather,
and a poorly functioning air conditioner –
we travel with windows open.
> *In an earlier time, in Kansas when vehicles were not air conditioned, we drove with windows open and the small vent window turned inward to direct moving hot air over our bodies, somehow despite the heat, creating the sensation of being cool and making the trip tolerable.*

San Miguel – We leave the Pan American Highway
driving inland toward the mountains and San Pedro.
> *The first time I saw the mountains in the distance across the high plain of Colorado they appeared as a bank of dark purple thunder clouds lying low on the horizon. Another half hour of driving and I realized – the clouds were the Rocky Mountains.*

Here the mountains have volcanic form; they seem close
and green.  Driving into the mountains –
    cities became towns;
        towns became villages;
            villages become communities.
The highway narrows – potholes, washouts, steep grades, dirt,
mud holes.  We exit the van and walk to prevent the vehicle
from disappearing into the abyss
of brown liquid filling the pot holes.
Hallelujah!!!  A pickup truck offers a ride.  We jump into the
bed of the pickup and ride

standing up holding onto the roll bar
as we bounce over the
    steepest,
        roughest,
            most washed out part of the road
after which we renew our journey in the van.
> When I worked on the farm we often rode in the bed of the pickup truck. Wind blowing through our hair as the truck sped down the highway was much better than sitting in the hot cab. It provided an unhindered view of meadowlarks, tumbleweeds, and gently rolling wheat fields.

## II

The road becomes less steep; we slowly inch through more mud holes, shifting into lower gear to climb the still rough terrain.
Beautiful vistas of lush seemingly untouched mountains unfold. Power poles and electric lines become extinct.
    Destination reached!

Los campesinos y las campesinas day to day
eke out a subsistence living; from one generation to the next, seldom venturing far from the community.
Visitors from the north, a rarity, are cause for celebration –
        fireworks,
             singing,
                dancing
before settling into the work of accompaniment –
being with and living with, sharing, and walking alongside those in the community.
        Stepping back in time
        little changed through the ages,
        life of the campesino.

### III

La casa del campesino –
Depends on available material:
>bamboo, adobe, mud, tin, clay tile roofs,
>sometimes cement floors
>>two, three, sometimes four rooms –
>>a room strung with hammocks for sleeping
>>a kitchen with clay hearth and open fire to cook
>>sometimes a room for storage
>>a porch for gathering

Apart from la casa, a brick and concrete outhouse,
designed when used correctly
to reduce smell and enhance composting.
>Climb rocky terrain
>then repel first cement step;
>arrive at outhouse

Diet –
>Breakfast – tortillas and beans with coffee
>Lunch – tortillas, rice and beans, occasionally cheese
>Supper – tortillas, rice and beans, sometimes plantains
>Special occasion picnic – tortillas, rice and beans, plantains, boiled eggs

### IV

What does the Lord require? Justice, mercy and humility
accomplished by being at the disposal of our God.
Accompanying those who are oppressed and vulnerable.

Hiking steep trails we visit las casas of community members:
Listen to joys and achievements –
>more protein in their diet,
>increased crop productivity,
>stabilization of food supply,
>micro loans to help farmers plant their crops, and

   scholarships for students to complete high school
   and college
Listen to sorrows and concerns –
   immigration,
   illness,
   death.
Discuss ways in which further investment might be channeled
   scholarships
   micro loans.

       V
Embedded in the trails we tread, an undercurrent in the life
of the community, is the war that ended a generation ago.
Most over age forty participated in the revolution as part
of the rebel force.
  Soldiers
    Cooks
      Messengers
        Caregivers of children left behind
Battle scars remain part of the fabric of their lives.
Some still carry the haunting violence of the conflict.
Many died in the conflict,
  some in battle,
    others of disease,
      others victims of massacres
      carried out by government forces
        in an effort to erode the will of the
        rebels.
Killing friends and loved ones inflames the passions of war.
Today rebel combatants will say – too many died;
change should come through peaceful dialogue.
But their party now incorporated into the government,
rules the country.
The people of San Pedro say their relationship
with North Americans is possible because of the outcome
of the war.

## VI

After the war,
    age old cycles of plenty and scarcity returned
        and circled in the life of San Pedro.
The threat of food scarcity and starvation loomed
and consumed the focus of the community.

    Vicious cycle
    Feast and famine
    Resources needed
    To examine

    What was required
    To undergird
    The food supply
    And thus be spurred

    To construct
    And think ahead
    Structures, methods
    Ensuring daily bread

    Silos storing corn
    Ponds containing fish
    Food supply stabilized
    Now other things for which to wish

## VII

Campesino life, ageless –
Subsistence farming –
    Corn, beans, and sugar cane
Housing structures –
    Different material, form the same
Diet –
    Corn and beans

Social life –
> By all means
> Kin and family
> Gather round
> In community
> They are bound.

Morning chore –
> Dawn breaks
> A fire to make
> Water boils
> Woman toils
> By clay oven
> In clothes hand woven
> Grinding corn
> In early morn
> Pat, pat, pat
> Tortillas flat
> Made traditional way
> Enough for the day

## VIII

Life in San Pedro is on the cusp of changing –
Some go to America,
Remittances – lifeblood for families left behind –
extra cash, money that lifts beyond the subsistence life.

Others continue their education
through high school and college.
New graduates bring new ideas,
    demand a different style of living,
        raise expectations, and
            open new doors.

## **remember poverty**

remember the time after the war?
remember jobs were plentiful
and people had money remember?
we bought a house on the edge of town
with an acre of ground
for a garden remember?
remember father bought
a new Montgomery Ward's tractor
and an ancient corn planter?
remember he operated the tractor
while mother operated the planter?
remember we played in the dirt
building roads and towns
in the corn, beans, and potatoes?
remember that garden
fed us
corn and beans
and peas and potatoes and
strawberries and grapes remember?
remember mother working
over the hot stove
canning the summer produce?
remember we ate that produce
all winter?
remember father was laid off
from his job and had to find
another job that paid less?
remember he was bitter about the
demotion and he soon was laid off
from that job because the mill closed?
remember he was depressed?
he could not find a job

sometimes tempers rose
and anger spat remember?
mother worked some
and remember at the end of each week
after the paycheck was cashed
they would count their money
and put a tenth back? remember to
give to the church regardless
of how little it was?
remember we always went to church
where we had cousins?
remember one large family of cousins
lived in the country
too far out for a casual visit?
remember when we visited
their tar shack house
we thought they were poor?
remember accidently stepping in one
of their open sewer line
caused stinky feet remember?
remember father ate
bread and milk and honey for dinner?
he thought we did not
have money for other food,
remember we had three sets of clothes
one good set for church
one set for school
and the old clothes for play? remember
we had to change into them
when we came home
from school?
remember father stopped
paying the house payments
but remember we did not have
to move out because remember
the loan was from our grandmother?

remember we did not
think we were poor
but remember we did not
have enough money
so remember we sold the house
and rented using the money
from the sale to pay the rent?
remember grandma
told us to repay
when we eventually got the money?
remember we repaid
grandma's estate when she died?
mother received nearly nothing
in the settlement remember?

James Burkett

# March of Terror

Mangled peaches, crushed
'til the juice runs red;
their mothers put to the axe.

Blackened pegs protrude,
vestiges from hell, smoldering
amid charred ruins.

"Terrorize them,"
the words of the
commander in chief.
No peach tree remains.

Lost in the wilderness
hungry and alone;
eat the fire to fill
the burning in the soul.

# One Breath Away

Regardless of age
    race
        gender
            wealth
                status in the community,
We,
    living creatures,
        are
            always
                one breath away
  From death.

James Burkett

# Night Without End

Will the long night
Ever come to an end?
For what reason
Should I leave my bed
To face the cold,
The storms
With foggy acumen
And sluggish guile,
My feet sinking
In the quicksand
Of meaninglessness,
Hanging tenaciously
And gripping tightly
To any thread of purpose?

The veil of gloom
Descends on my being;
Boredom stalks me.
I pass the days
In robotic habit,
In melancholic occupation
Awaiting sun down
And the passing
Of another day,
Each longer
And more drear
Than the previous one,
Each filled
With the nothingness
Of life.

Oh that the dark
Would envelope me
And carry me away
To more pleasant shores
Of warmth and light.

James Burkett

# Life

Live as though you
Will live forever;
Die as though you
Are going to a grand party

## Seventh Cousins

On a warm summer afternoon at the Farmer's Market,
I struck up a conversation
with an Amish man selling his vegetables
and cuts of Longhorn Steer meat. He proudly reported
the meat has a lower fat content than buffalo.
I inquired where he lives. "Near Romulus," he replied.
But he added that he used to live in Pennsylvania.
"Oh, where?" I asked. He told me it was near
a small obscure town in north central PA.
"In the Big Valley?" I asked. His eyes lit up.
He wanted to know how I knew about the Big Valley.

When one descends from Amish community
and attends to genealogy, the Big Valley becomes
a book mark. The conversation turned
to my Amish ancestors. I recited
the surnames of a number of those hearty
pioneers of the eighteenth century – Miller, Troyer,
Yoder, Zook – a litany of Amish names. His ancestors –
same surnames. He would have to look up
their given names. I told him about a book
of Amish genealogy. He did not know the book.

Next week I loaned him a copy
and pointed out my ancestors
listed in the book.
Several weeks later I saw him again at Market.
We talked about the book. He reported that he
found the genealogy book very interesting. He found
all his ancestors listed in it. And he added
with a smile and a twinkle in his eye,
"We are about seventh cousins."

James Burkett

# Tribe

From a young age I experienced the
  values
      beliefs
           customs
                and traditions
of our tribe. They wrapped me in their familiarity,
giving comfort, consistency, and a
perspective from which to see the world. The tribe
was home with all its love and spats.
For nearly seventy years I lived with the tribe.
We ate together; we sang together;
we listened to each other; we encouraged each other;
we worshiped together; we gave
a helping hand to each other.

I no longer live with the tribe. Its beliefs
too confining, its traditions too smothering.
But the tribe still lives with me. Its values guide
and its customs ring familiar. Unless I reveal
my identity, folks do not associate me with the tribe.
  I blend in.
      I often choose
           to not disclose my association.

Frequently outsiders speak about the tribe,
speculating about their distinct customs,
or lauding their values,
or wondering how the belief system originated.
Most of the time the conversations on which I eaves drop
are filled with respect and admiration
for the tribe and its members. However, in some
conversations overheard I detect strands of subtle

disapproval of the difference between the speakers
and the tribe.  Other times folks are harsh and angry
that the differences demand accommodation.
Always when people talk about the tribe I find myself
carefully listening and feeling a muted defensiveness
    for those with whom I
        no longer live.

James Burkett

# When an Old Man Dies a Library Burns

I open my mouth to speak
A flock of turkeys fly out
Confused, bewildered
They circle and drop

I think, "What a dunce,
  What a fool,
      What a clown,
          What a circus!"

Experiences and knowledge
      Are tucked away in my memory.
Owls, not turkeys should emerge.

It may not be possible to share all that I know
      and have experienced.
Items are tucked away in the back corners of my mind,
      long forgotten and not readily revealed.

Elegant spoken words drift around my mind
And need to be shared.
But looking into my voice box
I see only turkeys.

When an old man dies; a library burns.

# Mervin

Son of pioneers
Tiller of the soil
Sower of righteous intent

Soft spoken and kind
Sunday school teacher
Wise community leader

Expanding family
Sharing tribal heritage
Adopting twin boys

Giving constant care
To stricken partner
Until life's journey ended

Your leathery tanned face
From years in the sun
Riding an old tractor

Belies current plight
Now in padded room
Overtaken by the years

James Burkett

# Quietus

Should the tentacles of time or disease
Stretch out their clammy fingers
And grip my being in their icy lock
Ravaging body, judgment, thoughts, and communication
Creating words
Untimely uttered and ill spoken
Or acts ill conceived and misguided
Which inflict baneful mischief
And create grievous hurt
And prevail in opposition to my character
That thou has't known,
A character of noble intention
Desirous of peace and good will to all
Filled with compassion and love for family and neighbors
Yet prone to fail in achieving intent
Allowing self centeredness, and greed to obstruct,
Will you listen beyond the words
And see behind the actions
That despite my current condition
I love and cherish each of you,
And desire that you go on about your business
Without fretting about the state of my being.
For I approach that time
When one's grip on the discourse of common events
Becomes corrupted and distorted
By the failing of acumen and sagacity
Compounded by the loss of facility and valor
And my lot in life will be to but languish
Until the owl calls my name.
To you whom I have held near to my heart
When that time comes, allow the wise one precedent
And refrain from heroic deeds

To intervene in the cycle of life
That would prolong the wait
For passage through the dark tunnel
Where I shall lie down
With the millions who have traveled thus before.
Scoundrels and kings
The wise and the holy
Those of ancient seasons and those recently awake
Shall be my comrades
And I shall have no need to fret for lack of companionship.
I know that just as I have traversed that dark tunnel
You too will join the multitudes
And come to lie by my side.
So when that time comes for me to join the congregation
In that abstruse domain
And find my abode among those who reside therein
Allow me to honorably approach my bed
And lie down in peace.

James Burkett

# Looking Out the Window
## (from my seat in the airplane)

Over distance, haze
Air, an opaque misty shroud
This is what we breathe?

High mountains below
Expansive blue skies above
I float in between.

In the dark night sky
Ancient mysteries unveil,
I gaze out in awe.

## ABOUT THE AUTHOR

James Burkett spent his entire career working with emotionally and behaviorally challenged children and their families. After retiring he moved with his wife to the Finger Lakes region in New York to be near grandchildren. He loves spending summers outdoors and goes through the summer seasons barefooted, wearing sandals only when footwear is required. He has traveled to all of the states in the United States except Alaska. And he hopes to travel there in the next future.

Made in the USA
Columbia, SC
15 December 2018